WHY AND HOW
I WAS BORN

THIRD IN THE SERIES OF
THE LITTLE ME AND THE GREAT ME

A Story of Birth

Part One   JEAN LEARNS HOW GOD PLANNED FOR HER COMING

Part Two   THE HONOR OF BEING CHOSEN OUT OF MILLIONS.

Part Three   THE MIRACLE OF BIRTH.

Part Four   PARENTS SAY "WE NEED HELP IN THIS SENSITIVE AREA."

The "ME" Books

Published by The Partnership Foundation
Capon Springs, West Virginia

THE LITTLE ME AND THE GREAT ME SERIES

Book 1: The Seven Secrets

Book 2: My Secret Power

Book 3: Why and How I Was Born

by
LOU AUSTIN

assisted by his wife and family and a host of friends, parents, teachers, physicians (psychiatrists and pediatricians), psychologists and sociologists; with particular thanks due his twelve-year old granddaughter, Bonnie McKeown

illustrated by
CHARLES DUNN

Copyright © 1963 by
The Partnership Foundation. Printed in the United States of America
Library of Congress catalog card number 63-12224

OR PARENTS, TEACHERS AND ALL WHO LOVE CHILDREN

—"Her children arise up and call her blessed."—Prov. 31:28.

When we leave God out of the picture, we miss the glory and the meaning of His truly priceless gift—procreation. Reverently should we appreciate that in this vital matter, God has made us, in a very real sense, co-creators with Him.

When a layman without training in psychiatry, psychology or sociology feels ᵢpelled to undertake a story on a subject as delicate as this one, the indulgent ader is due an explanation.

The fact that the author is a grandfather with four children and fifteen andchildren only partially accounts for the inner compulsion which gave him ᵢ rest until this book was published.

What really triggered WHY AND HOW I WAS BORN was a visit to the ᵢain library of one of our largest cities. We had gone there in confident search ᵢ a proper and satisfying answer to the oft-raised question of children, ᵢow was I born?"

At the main counter of the Children's Division of the library, we asked ᵣ books on the subject. A librarian reached beneath the counter and produced ₙ books. Surprised, we asked why the books were kept there. The answer: ᵥe do not allow these books out where children can get at them."

Taken aback, we asked, "But does not this defeat the very purpose of such ᵢ book? Shouldn't the child be made to feel that the whole birth process is ᵢrt of a simple and natural plan of the Creator to people His earth?" The ᵢswer came rather embarrassedly, "We found that the children often deface ₑ illustrations. Also, parents don't want their children to have these books ᵣen they are not present with them."

An examination of the books revealed that without exception they were ᵢological explanations, well written and in good taste. They went into much ₑtail, both in illustrations and descriptions. No doubt, books such as these ₑ needed and serve a purpose. We felt, however, that something should ₑcede this kind of explanation—something that would bring the Creator ₜo the picture with His plan of Love and Family Life,—something in the way ᵢ a bridge to link the mystery of life with scientific fact.

Unless the Creator's part in a child's birth is made clear to the inquiring child—and with it, God's plan of Love and Family Life—the child can get the idea that humans reproduce in response to the purely physical urge commonly attributed to animals. To ignore the spiritual quality in humans when informing children of this highly sensitive procedure is to risk great harm.

It is not enough to cite the "birds and bees" as an example. God's plan for human beings involves His own participation (as the Creative Spirit of selfless love) in the ecstasy of mating. When God is left out, the entire process is devoid of the spiritual quality which was the primary reason for the creation of Man.

To make sure that we were right in this belief, we followed the practice found so successful with the first book in this series, THE LITTLE ME AND THE GREAT ME. This was to test the manuscript with teachers, parents and children before publishing the book. Our tests with the manuscript of WHY AND HOW I WAS BORN were, however, on a much wider scale. We felt that a story dealing with a subject as delicate and vital as this should not be considered ready for publication until thoroughly tested and found acceptable to children as well as to the experts.

So, the manuscript was submitted to more than five hundred parents and teachers, including psychiatrists, pediatricians and sociologists. It was also read to and by several hundred children, ranging in ages from seven to seventeen. The psychiatrists had assured us that the actual reaction of children to the story before publication would prove invaluable, and we found this to be so.

Results of Tests

The facts: Children took the forthright explanation of sex as they would accept any other fact in education. There was none of the embarrassment that often prevails with grown-ups when asked pertinent questions by children. (Incidentally, our tests confirmed what the experts had told us, that upwards of 90% of parents do not come to grips with these facts with their children.

Because the story was completely enveloped in an atmosphere of God's plan of Love and Family Life, the children found it easy and natural to accept.

Even in cases where children had first picked up rather unwholesome details from other youngsters, the reading of the manuscript of WHY AND HOW I WAS BORN seemed to resolve their doubts and overcome their distorted notions. Typical of this was the comment of an unusual twelve-year old boy, who had first picked up "the facts of life" in the way most boys do, "I think everyone not only children should read the story. I believe they would have a whole new outlook toward why people get married not just to have a good time but to enrich God's earth by bearing children."

We learned also, to our great satisfaction, that parents were helped in ways other than having their children learn the truth about their birth in an uplifting way. They were reminded that the birth of a child is proof of God's plan for true Love and Family Life, thus inspiring a more loving and understanding relationship.

As a consequence of our tests, the manuscript was revised again and again. I warmly acknowledge my debt to the many parents, educators and other professional people—with particular thanks to the children—who helped with their suggestions and answers. I owe much to my wife and children and grandchildren. The ease and naturalness with which two of my granddaughters (age 10 and 12) discussed with me every phase of the birth process as presented in this book, confirmed my belief that under the proper circumstances, children will accept the story of how they were born as naturally as they do other events in their lives.

The parents who had their children read the manuscript were grateful and in many cases relieved. Grateful, for the natural way in which their children took the revelations on sex; relieved, that they had been able to discharge an obligation to their children with such an inspiring effect. Some parents reported that at first they were reluctant to allow their children to read the manuscript, "but after they reacted so naturally to it, we recognized that our trouble was our inability to see things the way children see them. The only way to get their true reaction was to have them read the story."

Wrote one nine-year old boy: "It answers all the questions I want to know." Among the questions we asked children was, "What part of the story meant most to you?" The most frequent answer: "God chose me out of millions." Revelations about sex were secondary to the fact that God wanted them and chose them to be born.

We learned also that the child's ties to his father and mother were greatly strengthened. Without exception, every child responded in the affirmative to the question, "Do you think the story will create a greater love and respect in the child for his parents?"

God, Love and Family.

Even the most learned student of psychiatry, psychology or theology can not presume to have more than a glimpse of God's infinite wisdom. To try to give too many details to a child is not wise. There is much to the mystery of life that none can understand, let alone explain.

Perhaps a feeling of awe contributes to the reluctance of many parents to answer forthrightly their child's natural curiosity as to how he was born. Many a parent, genuinely concerned about giving his child proper understanding as to how he came to be, knows that he is dealing with something so complex and deep that he feels inadequate to explain it properly. Particularly is this so, where the parent has not been given, as a child, the kind of understanding he would now like to pass on to his child.

Biological facts are not enough. Indeed, if they are not presented as a part of the whole spiritual concept of family life, biological facts can be harmful. Anyone doubting this should ponder why prudently managed libraries find it necessary to keep such books hidden from children.

Recent years show a marked increase in "illegitimacy." (Really, there are no illegitimate children—only illegitimate parents.) Young people are uncertain and uneasy about how they should behave with one another. Lack of understanding about sex is often at the bottom of this situation. The children's written reactions to the manuscript offer convincing evidence that the best explanation on sex for the young child is the simple one enfolding the act with God, Love and Family.

In her opinion of the manuscript of WHY AND HOW I WAS BORN, a 15-year-old girl wrote, "I feel that if a story such as this would be read or told to children when they are old enough to understand, there would be fewer teenagers in trouble at the prime of their life."

A parent (and grandfather) in his written comment on the manuscript stated, "This book is badly needed. Unless the subject is discussed properly with a child before he learns it in the wrong way outside the home, there is a strong possibility the child will build up a guilt complex, with all its problems, that will be there for the rest of his life. This results in tensions, anxiety and many other emotions, all of them unpleasant."

When grown-ups squirm at the thought of discussing sex with children, it suggests that there may be something wrong about sex. And to suggest that there is something wrong about sex is to imply that there is something wrong about God, the Creator of sex.

We are living in a world where God's part in our creation and in our daily lives is being de-emphasized in the adoration of man's scientific achievements. Alas, we are worshipping the creature instead of the Creator, seemingly unaware that it is the Creator who keeps the creature's heart beating and his mind working.

We miss the glory and the meaning of God's truly priceless gift—procreation—when we leave God out of the picture. Reverently should we appreciate that in this vital matter, God has made us, in a very real sense, co-creators with Him. Even if no offspring is contemplated, an awareness of God's presence and participation (as the Creative Spirit of selfless love) in the physical union of husband and wife is essential to its completeness and ecstasy.

Emerson reminds us "The highest revelation is that God is in every man . . . That which shows God in me fortifies me. That which shows God out of me makes me a wart and a wen. There is no longer a necessary reason for my being."

We owe it to children to teach them, early in life, of the duality of their nature: each is part human, part divine. We need revive the old but neglected truth that there are two forces, two wills in every person: one—the will of the human self, the other—the will of the divine self. Tests with thousands of children during the past six years have demonstrated that a child as young as 2½ can grasp the idea that he has both a Little ME and a GREAT ME, and that he can choose which ME he wants to be.

We rightly teach our children self-reliance, but do not make its true meaning clear. Emerson explained: "Self-reliance, the height and perfection of man is reliance on God. If we should ask ourselves what is this self-respect, it would carry us to our highest problems. *It is our practical perception of the Deity in man* . . . and the question ever is, not what you have done or forborne, but *at whose* command you have done or forborne it." When it becomes second-nature to a child to seek the guidance of the divine part of his nature, normal and healthy reactions to all matters, including sex, can be predicted.

Finally, from the children's reactions to WHY AND HOW I WAS BORN, it is crystal clear that the most meaningful thing in the story to each child is the assurance that he was chosen and that there is a purpose to his life.

THE AUTHOR

IMPORTANT FOR PUBLIC SCHOOL USE

This nation believes in God. The phrase "under God" as used by Lincoln, was recently unanimously adopted by Congress, in the Pledge of Allegiance. God is non-sectarian.

Because questions as to the nature of God may lead to sectarian interpretation, the child raising any such question should be referred to his parents and church for the answer.

TO THE YOUNG READER

Before you read this book, you should be familiar with the first of THE LITTLE ME AND THE GREAT ME series, which tells of the Seven Secrets. In case you do not know them, here are

THE SEVEN SECRETS

1. The first secret is that everyone has two MEs, a Little ME and a GREAT ME. The Little ME is selfish, always wants to be first. No one loves the Little Me. THE GREAT ME is kind and unselfish. Everyone loves The GREAT ME.

2. The second secret is that I can choose between the Little ME and THE GREAT ME. I can be whichever ME I choose.

3. The third secret is how to make the Little ME go away. I blow out the Little ME like I blow out the candle on a birthday cake.

4. The fourth secret is that I can breathe in THE GREAT ME.

5. The fifth secret is that THE GREAT ME is GOD's Partner.

6. Secret number six is that God is my Partner and His Spirit is always with me.

7. The seventh secret is how I know that God is my Partner and His Spirit is always with me. I give a good blow (like blowing out the candle on a birthday cake). Then I close my mouth and pinch my nose tight. Very soon, I have to let go of my nose. Why? Because I must have God's air. I can't do without God's air. I can't do without God. God's Spirit comes in with the air I breathe. That's how I know that God's Spirit is always with me.

Everyone has 2 MEs

A little me

and a GREAT ME

You can choose which Me.

you can blow out the *little* Me

and
breathe in the GREAT ME

WHY AND HOW I WAS BORN

". . . . the door opened and in came Peter, Jean's teenage brother. Jean had to tell him. "Pete, Mom just told me the story of how I was born." Peter corrected her. "You mean why and how you were born, don't you? Dad told it to me when I was about your age, Jean.". . His mother said, "There is no more beautiful story than why and how we are born." From Page 33

"Mommy, tell me the story of how I was born." Jean had just returned from school with two friends.

"But Jean, I've already told you," her mother answered.

"I want Mary and her brother to hear it."

"Don't you think their own mother should tell them?"

Mary giggled, "My mother laughs and says a stork brought me." Her brother John said, "My dad says I'm too young to know."

Jean's mother thought a moment; then answered, "I believe that Mary and John should hear the story from their own parents. Besides, they would first have to learn about THE LITTLE ME AND THE GREAT ME. That's the main part of our story."

Jean said eagerly, "I can lend them my book."

"That's a good idea," her mother agreed. "It will be a good start for them."

"I've got another idea," Jean said. "Let's ask Grandpa to write a story about how we are born, like he wrote THE LITTLE ME AND THE GREAT ME. Then all children can learn from it."

That is how this story came to be written. It is told much the way Jean's mother told it to her.

* * * * *

Part One

It was a rainy afternoon—just right for a heart-to-heart chat between mother and daughter as they sat alone at home.

"Jean, three words tell the story of how you came to be born: GOD, LOVE and FAMILY. Remember these three words when you hear people talk about how babies are born."

"But those three words don't tell me how I was born."

"They will tell you *why* you were born. It is even more important for you to know *why* you were born than *how* you were born."

"Do the two words go together—*why* and *how?*"

"Yes, they do. They go together, but *why* comes first."

"Why does it?"

"Because it gives the reason for your being born. You like to know the reason for things, don't you? You usually ask 'Why?' when you want to know the reason."

"Then tell me *why* I was born."

The story begins with God—the Creator of all things."

"Did God make everybody?"

"Including you. You will learn that He went to special trouble to make you. God wanted you here."

"How do you know that?"

"Years before you were born, God planned for your coming."

"How?"

"He arranged for your daddy and mommy to meet, to love one another and to be married. God planted the spirit of love deep in our hearts, one for the other."

"The way you love me and I love you?"

"Love between Daddy and Mommy is a different kind of love from the love between parents and children, or between friends and relatives."

"Are there different kinds of love?" asked Jean.

"Yes, it's too bad the English language has only one word for the different kinds of love. The Greeks had four or five words for the different kinds of love."

"Why did God make a different kind of love for you and Daddy?"

"It's the special kind of love God planned for the building of the human family. To carry out His plan, God planted seeds of love in Daddy and me to start a family. In a family, there are a father, a mother and children."

Jean exclaimed, "Mommy, you've mentioned all three words: God, Love and Family."

"There will be a fourth word to add: the word Me, meaning yourself."

"Then there are four words that I should remember: God, Love, Family and Me."

"Yes, Jean, and I hope you will be sure that the word Me means THE GREAT ME."

"I know, Mommy. I don't want to be the Little ME." But Jean was eager to hear more of the story. "After God planted seeds of love in you and Daddy, then what?"

"Then God directed Daddy to transfer his seeds of love to me."

"How?"

"That comes under 'how' and I'm not yet finished with 'why.' God begins everything with a seed. Often the seed is so tiny you can't see it."

"Some seeds you can see—the seeds we plant for flowers."

"But the seed which started you was too small to be seen. First, you should know that God is Love, and since He is true

GOD

begins everything with a
SEED

Love, He gives things with a loving and generous hand. Often He gives out millions of seeds even if He expects only one seed to grow."

"Why?"

"Because He is loving and generous. When you see a field of dandelions go to seed, millions and millions of seeds are blown into the air. Only a few of these seeds grow."

"What happens to the other seeds?"

"The others may fall onto rock or into water or some place where they cannot grow. Some are eaten by birds."

"But the seeds God wants to grow—they grow, don't they?"

"They are the only ones that grow—the ones God permits to grow. If God allowed all the seeds to grow, we'd have nothing but dandelions."

Jean was thoughtful. "The acorns that fall from the oak tree near the school—what happens to them?" she asked. "They have seeds in them, don't they?"

"If God allowed all these acorns to grow, we'd have nothing but oak trees. So only a few take root and grow."

"What happens to the rest that don't grow?"

"Some serve as food for small animals; some crumble into the ground, making the soil richer for other things to grow."

Jean's eyes sparkled as she thought of something. "How about all the seeds in a watermelon? What a watermelon party we could have if they all grew into watermelons!"

Her mother smiled with her. "Yes, but there wouldn't be room for much else."

"Why does God make so many seeds that never grow?"

"As I said, He is a loving and generous Creator. He wants to make sure that life goes on and on and on."

"I don't understand," said Jean.

"Life can continue only if new seeds are being planted all the time. Babies have to be born every day all over the world

f ALL
watermelon seeds grew - we would
have nothing but WATERMELONS

if life is to go on the way God planned it."

"I don't see why He has to waste millions of seeds just to grow one."

"Well, I think that there is something behind this which God wants us to realize. God wants His children always to remember, no matter what happens, that He Himself chose each to be born."

Jean looked puzzled. Her mother said, "I'll try to make it clearer for you. Here is where the *why* runs into the *how*. We're coming soon to where you learn how you were born."

Jean's eyes were fixed on her mother. Quiet but alert, she waited to hear more.

* * * * *

GOD creates many seeds for just ONE to grow

Part Two

THE HONOR OF BEING CHOSEN OUT OF MILLIONS

After a moment's pause, Jean's mother continued. "It's wonderful how God plans so far ahead. He planned the family so that life would go on. He planned love between a man and a woman so that they would marry and have a family."

"Is that why God made girls different from boys?"

"You do understand, Jean. Yes, God made girls different from boys so that there would be more and more families. Long before a baby is born, God decides whether it is to be a girl or a boy."

"But the father and mother don't know till the baby is born whether it's a girl or a boy," said Jean.

"That's right. The doctor looks at the front of the baby. If there's something below the navel no bigger than a little finger (which doctors call penis) the doctor calls out, 'It's a boy.' Behind the penis is a small sac. In this sac are what doctors call testicles. They grow the seeds for future babies."

Jean exclaimed, "And if there's nothing in front, the doctor calls out, 'It's a girl.' "

"If the doctor sees only a small opening (which he calls vagina) he knows it's a girl. When girls and boys grow up and near the age when they are allowed to vote, God causes them to think about marrying and raising a family."

"How does God tell them that?"

"When God wants to tell us something, He has His own way to do it. He speaks to us through our GREAT ME—God's Spirit in us."

"And God told you He wanted me to be born?"

"Yes, He did. In His own way, God told your father and me. A few years after Peter was born, God reminded us that He expected an addition to our family. As I told you, it is through the family that God planned for life to go on and on."

"And you did what God told you to do."

"Because we love and respect God, and because we wanted you to be born, we followed God's direction that very night."

"What did you do, Mom?" Jean was full of natural curiosity.

"We did just what God told us to do. God had arranged for the bodies of married people to fit and join one another, so that when Daddy and I lovingly put our arms around each other, we became as one. The penis entered the vagina, and the seeds of love were transferred from his body to mine."

"God wanted you to do this so that I could be born?"

"We were acting in partnership with God. This is His

divine plan for a man and a woman who love and marry."

"And was I born right away?"

"Not right away. After the love seeds (which doctors call sperm) are transferred, God takes over the whole thing Himself. From that time on, God does everything."

"What does He do?"

"Now, the *how* comes together with the *why* again. I told you how generous God is with His seeds."

"Like dandelion, acorn and watermelon seeds," said Jean.

"Yes. When God directed Daddy to transfer his seeds of love to me, God did not cause just one seed to be transferred; He caused millions of the tiny seeds to be transferred."

"Why so many if only I was to be born?"

"God has shown in many ways that His love for people is even greater than for plants and animals. But even more important, He did this to make sure you would understand, when you grew older, that He wanted *you* to be born, not any of the others."

"I don't understand," said Jean.

"Well, God knew that out of the many seeds from Daddy, He would choose just one seed to join with one of my love seeds (which doctors call an ovum). God chose these two seeds Himself, and joined them together as one seed or cell to stay and grow in my body."

"When God joined the two seeds together, He was choosing me to be born!" said Jean excitedly.

"Yes, God was choosing you."

"God chose me out of all those millions of seeds! What happened to the other seeds?"

"They were never used and were soon eliminated from my body. God wanted *you* to be born, not any one else that might have come from a union of other seeds."

"What would have happened if God chose two other seeds

out of
MILLIONS of SEEDS
GOD chose YOU to be born

and joined them together?" Jean was curious.

"Someone else would have been born, not you."

"Wouldn't that someone be me?"

"No, it wouldn't have been you any more than your brother or your sister is you. God wanted you to be born, not anyone else that He might have chosen. And He wanted you born at the time you were born."

"Why would He want me, I wonder?"

"If God wants you here, it must be that He plans for you to do something while you are here. Something worthwhile."

"Like what? To be famous?"

"Not necessarily, but it is something that only you can do. It must be, if He picked you out of millions. Doesn't it make you feel good to know that you are wanted? And to be wanted by God is the best thing there is."

"But I can't do anything by myself. I can't do anything big or famous."

"Not by yourself. But I have a wonderful secret for you. It belongs with the seven secrets of THE LITTLE ME AND THE GREAT ME."

"Which one is it?"

"When God joined the two seeds together and chose you to be born, He breathed into you with the breath of life, part of His own divine Spirit."

"I know," Jean said with a smile. "That's my GREAT ME."

"I hope you'll never forget that, Jean. God's Spirit is with you all the time, as your GREAT ME."

"Some kids say that God is up in Heaven."

"God's Spirit is everywhere, but most important of all, God's Spirit is within us. That's why God made us—to live in partnership with Him."

"I'll try to be a GREAT ME and do what God wants me to do. Must it be something great?" Jean sounded a little worried.

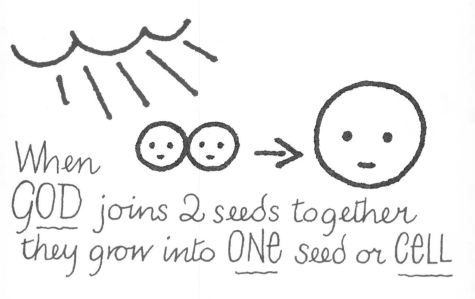

When **GOD** joins 2 seeds together they grow into **ONE** seed or **CELL**

"Not as some people think a thing great. It may be something simple, like being kind to others, but if it's what God wants you to do, He will think it great."

"I know I'll have to blow my Little ME out of the way. I won't be able to do what God wants me to do, if I'm a Little ME."

"But you're not a Little ME very often."

"I don't know why I act that way. I always feel better when I'm trying to be a GREAT ME."

Jean's mother put her arm lovingly around her, as she said, "You know, Jean, there is another reason for you to be a GREAT ME."

"What is that?"

"Now you know you carry the seeds of love within you so God can create babies through you. You will want to be a

GREAT ME for the sake of your babies."

"Some day I will have babies of my own!" There was wonder in Jean's voice as she realized this.

"That means you should also take care of your body and your mind. These are not only the temple for God's Spirit; they are also the temple for your own future babies."

"What is a temple, Mommy?"

"A temple is a home for God's loving Spirit."

Jean said thoughtfully, "I must take care of my body and mind because they are a home for God's Spirit."

"And also because—". A twinkle in her eye, Jean interrupted her mother, "And also because they will be a home for my own babies some day."

"Jean, I believe you do understand. I'm so glad that you do." With that, her mother drew Jean close to her.

"And I'm so glad that you and Daddy joined with God in wanting me to be born."

*   *   *   *   *

with every breath GO_D
breathes into you the GR_EAT M_E

Part Three

THE MIRACLE OF BIRTH

For a moment or two, mother and daughter sat close to one another in thoughtful silence. Then Jean had more questions. "You said God took over everything and did the whole thing Himself. What did He do?"

"Well, when God picked the one love seed out of millions of Daddy's, He joined it to one seed of mine, making the two seeds into one cell."

"That one was to be me, wasn't it?"

"No one else but you," her mother assured Jean. "At that time, you were only a little speck, too small to be seen."

Jean laughed. "I couldn't be seen anyhow, deep inside your body."

"No," her mother smiled. "You couldn't be seen anyhow."

"How long did I stay there before I was born?"

"Nine whole months. I carried you under my heart all that time, in a place called the womb, which God made just for that purpose. You were cradled in love, so each day you grew closer to my heart of hearts."

Jean looked up at her mother with a loving smile. Her mother went on, "And then came the day when I first felt you moving. That was a thrill."

"How did you start me moving?"

"I didn't. God did that."

"And I kept growing all the time?"

"Each month you grew bigger and stronger."

"Is that why mothers get big like Aunt Florence?"

"Yes, Aunt Florence is pregnant. That means she is going to have a baby. Growing a baby is all God's work, as I said. The way God looked after you when you were growing in my body seemed like a miracle."

"What did He do?"

"He arranged for you to receive from my body the nourishment you needed to grow. I was careful to eat the right foods, get lots of fresh air and rest."

"You were taking care of me while I was getting ready to be born, weren't you, Mom?"

"Yes, God was taking care of both of us. As if by magic, the food I ate was changed to blood and bone and muscle and brain for your body, Jean. Everything worked just right."

"Sounds like magic," said Jean. "How did you know when it was time for me to be born?"

"God let me know. He lets all mothers know. He told me when it was time for you to be born."

"How?" Jean persisted.

"There were some moments of pain, but these were forgotten in the happy thought that you would soon be born."

"What did you do then?"

"I told Daddy and he called the doctor."

"And the doctor helped me to be born?"

"The doctor was a big help, but it was God in His own way, who gently pushed you out of my body."

"Where did I come out?"

"The same place that you came in as a love seed. God arranged that. You came in as a seed of love and you came out as a child of love. It is the same love but in a different form."

"What was the first thing I did after I came out?"

"As soon as you got out into the air, you made an awful racket. That was after the doctor smacked your little bottom. Everyone laughed. We knew you were all right."

"Why did the doctor smack my bottom?"

"To get you to cry so as to breathe in air. That was your first breath, and like the rest of us, you've been coming to God every moment since for the breath of life."

Jean giggled. "And so I was born."

"And so you were born. God had worked one of His miracles."

"What do you mean, Mom?"

"Everyone got what he wanted. God got what He wanted: another child to live in partnership with Him. We got what we wanted: you. And you got what you wanted: life. That's a miracle, isn't it? It isn't often everyone gets what he wants."

"It's nice getting what you want."

"Sometimes God refuses us what we want because He knows it's not best for us. But He knew that having you born was best for all of us."

Jean was pleased. How soon did you give me something to

The MIRACLE

GOD got what HE wanted
WE got what WE wanted
YOU got what YOU wanted

eat?" she asked.

"Very soon. You nursed at mother's breast as long as I could feed you. That's another way in which God made girls different from boys. When you get a little older, you will notice your breasts getting fuller. That's to hold the milk for your babies some day. Only girls are made that way. It's one of the ways that show how far ahead the Creator prepares girls to become mothers."

"Are there other ways?"

"Yes. Also as you grow older, you will notice that about the same time each month, a little blood will be discharged from the vagina. This is known as the menstrual or monthly period."

"What's that for?"

"Here again, we learn how wonderfully the Creator lays plans for the creation of babies long in advance of their coming. Soon, God will cause a sort of nest to be prepared in your womb each month to receive and nourish the cell formed by the union of the two chosen seeds."

"Why so far ahead if I won't need it until I marry?"

"Probably because the Creator wants you to be fully prepared for the time when you marry. God expects you to make sure that only the seed from the right man will be the one to enter the nest."

"What happens to the nest if no cell is formed?"

"The Creator has arranged for the nest to be washed away."

"Why?"

"To make ready for the new nest that will be formed the next month. What you notice each month is the blood that made up the old nest."

"Tell me more about it, Mommy."

"I have a special book all about this for you, but the important thing to remember is that God is planning far ahead for you to be co-creator with Him in creating a baby. This monthly reminder is God's promise of the blessing of motherhood for you some day."

"Oh Mommy, that is beautiful."

"It *is* beautiful. It's a blessing that is *mine* right now, in having and loving you. It will be *your* blessing some day."

Once again Jean looked thoughtful. "But not everybody gets married and has babies, do they, Mom?"

"No, Jean. There are some men and women who do God's work in other ways than marrying and raising a family. Many of these good people give up the joy of having children but find a different joy in doing God's work in other ways."

"And how about Bobby? He's adopted."

"Well, there are some married people who, for reasons only God knows, are unable to have children of their own. Many of these couples adopt children who no longer have parents. These folks don't think of themselves as unusual, but they are."

"They must love children."

"Yes, and they must love God, because they go one step further to do His will. Just as God picked out the certain seeds to make the child, He caused these people to pick out the special child they wanted to adopt."

"Adopted children are chosen twice then, aren't they?"

"Yes, first by God alone, then by God and the new parents."

"It's another miracle, isn't it, Mom?"

"It must be a part of God's divine plan. These people are eager to make a home for the children, and God gives them the joy of being parents, which was their secret wish."

Jean had another thought. "There are twins in our school. How do twins happen?"

"Perhaps God, who gives us such a variety in other things, feels that every now and then, He should vary the practice of choosing just one seed."

"So He chooses two seeds?"

"He chooses two seeds (or sperms) to join with two ova to make fraternal twins, which may turn out to be one boy and one girl. Or He may divide into two the one cell He had just formed (of the daddy's sperm and the mommy's ova) and create identical twins who look alike and are of the same sex."

"Sounds like more of God's magic," said Jean.

"Well, God's ways are above magic as the heavens are above the earth; ways we often can not understand, let alone explain. But of this we may be sure, each child is precious to Him."

Jean was ready with another question. "How about Betty? She was born crippled. Why did God let that happen?"

"No one knows that answer. We who are well should be grateful that we have been blessed with health."

"I wish I could help Betty," said Jean thoughtfully.

"Perhaps you do. Crippled people don't want pity. You make her happy when you play with her and show her you love her."

"Betty never complains even if she can't do what we do."

"The way these people take their misfortunes . . . often winning despite their handicaps. . . ." Her mother did not finish the sentence.

"God helps them do that, doesn't He?"

"Yes. As you grow up, Jean, you're bound to meet with some troubles—we all do—but that's a good time to count your blessings."

"Why must we have troubles?"

"That's part of God's plan to grow. 'All sunshine makes a desert.' Just as rain is needed to make things grow, we need troubles to grow to be a GREAT ME."

"I don't like troubles."

"No one does. But look how God works. If Helen Keller had not been deaf and dumb and blind, she would not have been able to help the many other people who are deaf, dumb and blind. And Helen Keller has lived a very happy and useful life. Many people without handicaps have not been as happy or as helpful."

Jean asked gently, "They're all God's children like us, aren't they, Mommy?"

Putting her arms around her daughter, Jean's mother smiled down into the clear questioning eyes, as she said, "You make me so glad that God gave you to me as my daughter, and I'm grateful to Him, too, that you are what He made you to be."

"And I'm glad you're my mommy," Jean responded, snuggling close to her mother. The light of true love was shining in the eyes of both.

* * * * *

Part Four

The door opened and Jean saw her father come in. His face lighted up as he looked at mother and daughter.

"It looks like somebody loves somebody," he smiled. They smiled back. He leaned over and kissed them.

Jean said, "Somebody does love somebody. I love Mommy and she loves me."

"Where do I come in?" asked her father. "I love you both."

Jean laughed. "And we love you. Mommy just told me how I was born."

Her mother corrected her. *"Why* and *how* you were born."

"Why and how I was born," repeated Jean.

Her father explained that he had told that story to her older brother a few years ago. "Is it all clear now?" he asked Jean. "Are you happy?"

Jean got up and putting her arms around her father, exclaimed, "I'm as happy as I can be, Daddy. I'm happy that God wants me here."

"He surely does want you here," said her father, "and so do we. We wouldn't know what to do without you."

"Even when I'm a Little ME?" asked Jean, with a cute grin.

"You're not a Little ME very often."

"That's what I told her," said Jean's mother.

"I'm not a good loser. I like to win too much, I guess."

Her father comforted her. "I still say, Jean, you're a GREAT ME most of the time."

As Jean smiled up at her father, the door opened again and in came Peter, Jean's teenage brother.

Jean had to tell him. "Peter, Mom just told me the story of how I was born."

sometimes I'M a little me

Peter corrected her. "You mean *why* and *how* you were born, don't you?"

"That's right; you know the story, too."

"Dad told it to me when I was about your age, Jean." Turning to his father, Peter said, "It sure was a big help, Dad. I wouldn't want the goofy ideas some of the other kids have."

"They seem confused?" asked his father.

"Boy, are they mixed up! How come they never learned from their parents?"

"Their parents meant to tell them. Probably weren't sure when to tell them."

"Or how to do it," added mother. "This part of married life is so intimate and sacred, some parents hesitate to talk about it, even to their children."

"I bet they wouldn't hesitate if they heard their kids talk," said Peter. "Kids learn about birth one way or the other. Why not the right way, straight from their parents?"

"You feel the other way may cause them trouble?"

"It sure does." Peter had no doubts about it. "Even now, they'll whisper and snicker about things that seem natural to me."

His father looked thoughtful. "Are you trying to say that parents who do not pass the facts on to their children are really passing the buck?"

Peter was sure of himself. "Well, they may not mean to do that, but let's face it. I'm 13. If any parents think a kid can reach 13 without picking up stories somewhere about how he was born, they're kidding themselves."

"I'm sure you're right, Peter," his father agreed. "It's important that children learn the facts in the right way."

His mother said, "There is no more beautiful story than why and how we are born."

"I love it," Jean bubbled over. "I'm glad God chose me to be born. It makes me feel good to know that God is my Partner."

Her mother smiled. "When you say that, Jean, you are thanking God, and showing your respect for His divine plan."

"Does that mean I'm a GREAT ME?" Jean smiled back. "But I'm getting too old to go around blowing out the Little ME. How do you and Daddy get rid of the Little ME?"

"We quietly breathe out the Little ME and breathe in THE GREAT ME. That's why God divided breathing into two parts, out and in."

"Oh, you breathe out instead of blowing out. I'll try that. The Seventh Secret will help me remember," said Jean.

GOD planned LOVE
between man and woman so
they would marry and have
a FAMILY

"Which one is the seventh?" asked Peter.

"How I know that God's Spirit is always with me. First, I give a good blow." (Jean blew out.) "Then I close my mouth and pinch my nose tight." (Jean pinched her nose.)

"I remember now," said Peter. "In a little while you have to let go of your nose."

Jean let go of her nose. "Do you remember why?" she asked Peter. "Because God's air has to come in to me."

"Sure. And God's Spirit comes in with His air."

"That shows I can't do without God."

"It also proves you can't do without God's air." No sooner had Peter said this than a knowing look came into his face. He snapped his fingers. "Now I know what happened in that race last week."

His father looked at Peter wonderingly. "What do you mean, son?"

"Remember my telling you that I got out of breath and the other kids were passing me?"

"Yes, I recall that, but you didn't quit. You went on to make a good showing."

"Right. Suddenly I got my breath back."

"That was your second wind, Peter."

"Yes. That's what saved me."

"It gave you what you needed?" asked his dad.

"Well, it reminded me that God was my Partner and that He was with me. This gave me confidence. I was able to pick up speed."

Jean asked, "What about the guy who won and the other kids? God was their Partner, too, wasn't He?"

Her mother answered, "That's true. It's not too important who won, although it's nice to win. The really important thing is to know that God's Spirit is always with you."

"All I know," said Peter, is that as soon as I remembered that,

I felt better."

"That's what I mean," said Mother. People who don't know they have a GREAT ME never reach their best. We who do know, often forget and take God for granted."

"I guess we all take our Partner's help for granted," said Daddy. "When you understand that God is really your Partner, you'll learn to divide things into two parts: 1) things you can do yourself (with His help or permission); 2) things only your Partner can do for you."

Jean asked, "What do you mean, Daddy?"

Her mother answered. "It's as I told you, Jean. God lets us help in the planting of seeds, but growing is all His own doing."

Jean remembered. "Like a baby. The daddy and mommy help to plant the seeds, but only God can make the baby."

Her father nodded. "You're right, Jean. And only God can make the baby *grow*. We need God's help in everything.

Peter said, "Dad, I remember when you used to wheel Jean around, you said everybody should look at a new baby every day."

His mother explained, "That's because a baby is born filled with God's loving Spirit, and we can't help getting a little of it, too."

"God's Spirit is our GREAT ME, isn't it?" asked Jean.

"Yes," answered her dad. "What mother says is true, but what I had in mind was that every new baby should remind us that we were once that helpless. Even now, we can't do much without God's help. I don't keep my heart beating. God does that for me."

With a mischievous twinkle in her eyes, Jean turned to her brother and said, "Pete, Mom says that right after I was born, you came up to me and said, 'Tell me quick before you forget it, what does God look like?'"

Mom and Dad smiled while Jean giggled. Peter blushed.

some things I
can do for myself
(with GOD'S help or permission)

other things
only GOD can
do for me

"Aw," he said, "Mom must have read that somewhere." As if to change the subject, he asked, "How about our Little ME? Why did God give us one?"

"Yes," said Jean, "Why did He give us two MEs? They're always fighting, aren't they?"

"THE GREAT ME doesn't fight," replied Mother. "He simply waits for The Little ME to learn that the only way to be happy is THE GREAT ME's way."

"That's not easy," said Jean. "My Little ME likes to have its own way."

"That's true of all of us, but it doesn't take long to see that our own way gets us into trouble," said her dad. "When people quarrel and fight, it's their Little MEs trying to have their own way."

Jean was not satisfied. "Wouldn't it be better if God didn't give us a Little ME?"

Her father answered, "If God didn't give each of us a Little ME all our own, different from everyone else, we'd all be the same. We would be like puppets on a string, without freedom of choice."

Mother added, "And there would be no challenge to see whether we could change our Little ME into THE GREAT ME."

"That's right," Peter broke in. "Without our Little ME we'd be bored. It's always a challenge to win over the Little ME."

Father nodded in approval. "That's the real purpose of life— to make our two MEs into one. When we try to change our Little ME to THE GREAT ME, we show our thanks to God for His many blessings and at the same time, we find our own happiness."

Jean said, "I thank God for choosing me out of millions. I feel so good about that. I'm glad you and Mommy joined with God to have me born."

There was something special in Jean's happiness. She knew now not only *how* she had been born, but more importantly, *why.*

She had learned in the right way what every girl and boy should know.

* * * * *

That night, Jean had a few thoughts of her own to add to her usual prayers. "Thank you, God, for choosing me. I'll try to be a good partner to you. I want to be a GREAT ME like Daddy and Mommy—and Peter." Then remembering some things, "Well, they are, most of the time. Nobody can be a GREAT ME all the time."

Jean took a deep breath in and then she breathed out. "What an easy way to remember that God is always with me!" she thought.

When her parents came in later, as they did each night before retiring, they found Jean fast asleep. On her face was the sweetest, loveliest smile you'd ever want to see. Her parents stood there, hand in hand, with thankful hearts that they had been blessed with so happy a daughter.

Jean's mother whispered, "If every child knew that he was born to live in partnership with God, he'd grow up with peace in his heart."

"Yes," answered Jean's father, "and when people have peace in their hearts, there will be peace in the world."

END

SO, MY YOUNG READER, you know how this story came to be written. I hope you agree with Jean's mother that there is no more beautiful story than why and how we are born. Isn't it wonderful to know that God made you to be His Partner? For this purpose, He chose you out of millions.

Your GREAT ME—which is really God's Spirit in you—will help you be a good partner to God.

Your Little ME will try to make you believe that your happiness will depend on HOW MANY THINGS YOU HAVE. But your GREAT ME knows that the previous sentence is incomplete, because it should read that your happiness will depend on *HOW MANY THINGS YOU HAVE DONE FOR OTHERS.*

You can always trust your GREAT ME to guide you. Abraham Lincoln wrote, "Without the divine assistance (THE GREAT ME) I cannot succeed; with it, I cannot fail."

Happy living!

Lou Austin

P. S. If you would care to write me what this book means to you, I will try to reply to you promptly. Perhaps your parents have friends who would like to know of this book. You can write me at Capon Springs, West Virginia.

the GREAT ME
is GOD'S partner

QUESTIONS

as prepared by the author's granddaughters
Laurie McKeown (10) and Bonnie McKeown (12)

1. What four words tell how you came to be born?

2. What does God begin everything with?

3. Why does God give out millions of seeds when He expects only one
   to grow?

4. Why did God make girls and boys instead of just one sex?

5. Why did God pick you out of millions of seeds?

6. How long did Jean stay in her mother's body before she was born?

7. Why did Jean's mother call her birth a miracle?

8. Why should you take care of your body and mind?

9. Is God only in Heaven? Where is He?

10. Why does God give us a Little ME and a GREAT ME?

11. Is God your Partner when you're a Little ME?

12. How does God make use of troubles in His Plan?

13. How did Peter's Partner come to his help in the race?

14. About what age should boys and girls begin to think of marrying?

15. On what should your happiness depend? Finish this sentence:
    HOW MANY THINGS YOU HAVE . . .

All financial interest in this book, including royalties, is assigned to The Partnership Foundation, a non-profit organization, dedicated to furthering the concept of the Partnership of Man and Maker.

GOD IS MY PARTNER

words by
Lou Austin

music by
Lowell Mason

God is my Part — ner; He's with me now. He never leaves me,
He's my Lea — der now. I'll do my best to be More like THE
GREAT ME Breathing out my Lit tle ME Brings God near-er to me.
(breathe out)

2 God chose me to be born
He wants me here,
Wants me for His Partner
What an honor dear!
I must not let Him down
His Spirit's my GREAT ME.
Knowing that God's with me
Makes me strong and free!

3 God gave me a Little ME
all of my own
God's Spirit's my GREAT ME
I'm never alone
He lets me free to choose
Which ME I want to be
I'll try my best to be
God's true GREAT ME.

GOD IS MY PARTNER

(CONTINUED)

4 To be a GREAT ME
Is no easy thing,
But that's what I want to be
Then my heart will sing
I'll breathe out The Little ME
      (breathe out)
Breathe in THE GREAT ME
      (breathe in)
Knowing that God's with me
Makes me strong and free.

5 Some people may not know
They have a GREAT ME,
If I live like one
They may learn from me.
I'll do my best to be
A GREAT ME for all to see,
Then I'll be helping God,
As He is helping me.

6 God is my Partner,
He's with me now.
He knows what's best for me,
To His will I'll bow.
When trouble comes my way,
God's with me all the way.
Trouble helps me to grow
Nearer to God.

7   (pointing to your neighbor)
God is your Partner.
He's with you now.
That makes us brothers.
He's our Leader now.
When trouble comes your way,
Let me help you I pray.
Helping you helps me to grow
Nearer to God.

8   (joining hands, all)
God is our Partner
He's with us now.
He'll never leave us,
He's our Leader now.
We'll breathe out The Little ME
      (breathe out)
Breathe in THE GREAT ME
      (breathe in)
Every breath brings you and me
Nearer to God.